North American Birds

Bald Eagles

by Rachel Grack

Bullfrog Books

Ideas for Parents and Teachers

Bullfrog Books let children practice reading informational text at the earliest reading levels. Repetition, familiar words, and photo labels support early readers.

Before Reading

- Discuss the cover photo. What does it tell them?
- Look at the picture glossary together. Read and discuss the words.

Read the Book

- "Walk" through the book and look at the photos. Let the child ask questions. Point out the photo labels.
- Read the book to the child, or have him or her read independently.

After Reading

- Prompt the child to think more. Ask: Have you ever seen a bald eagle? Where was it? What was it doing?

Bullfrog Books are published by Jump!
5357 Penn Avenue South
Minneapolis, MN 55419
www.jumplibrary.com

Library of Congress Cataloging-in-Publication Data

Names: Koestler-Grack, Rachel A., 1973– author.
Title: Bald eagles / by Rachel Grack.
Description: Minneapolis, MN: Jump!, Inc., [2025]
Series: North American birds | Includes index.
Audience: Ages 5–8
Identifiers: LCCN 2023050178 (print)
LCCN 2023050179 (ebook)
ISBN 9798892131018 (hardcover)
ISBN 9798892131025 (paperback)
ISBN 9798892131032 (ebook)
Subjects: LCSH: Bald eagle—North America—
Juvenile literature.
Classification: LCC QL696.F32 K626 2025 (print)
LCC QL696.F32 (ebook)
DDC 598.9/43—dc23/eng/20231109
LC record available at https://lccn.loc.gov/2023050178
LC ebook record available at https://lccn.loc.gov/2023050179

Editor: Katie Chanez
Designer: Emma Almgren-Bersie

Photo Credits: BirdImages/iStock, cover, 3; Locomotive74/Shutterstock, 1, 22; Albert Beukhof/Shutterstock, 4; JamesBrey/iStock, 5; ca2hill/iStock, 6–7; Byron Layton/Shutterstock, 8–9; Thomas Torget/Shutterstock, 10, 23bl; igorkov/iStock, 11; Ufocus/Shutterstock, 12–13, 23br; Richard Seeley/Shutterstock, 14; Martin Smart/Alamy, 15; predrag1/iStock, 16–17, 23tl; htrnr/iStock, 18–19; Jeffrey Schwartz/Shutterstock, 20–21; showcake/Shutterstock, 23tr; GlobalP/iStock, 24.

Printed in the United States of America at Corporate Graphics in North Mankato, Minnesota.

Table of Contents

White Head

Look up!

A bald eagle is in a tree.

It has long wings.

It flies!

It has a white head.

It has a brown body.

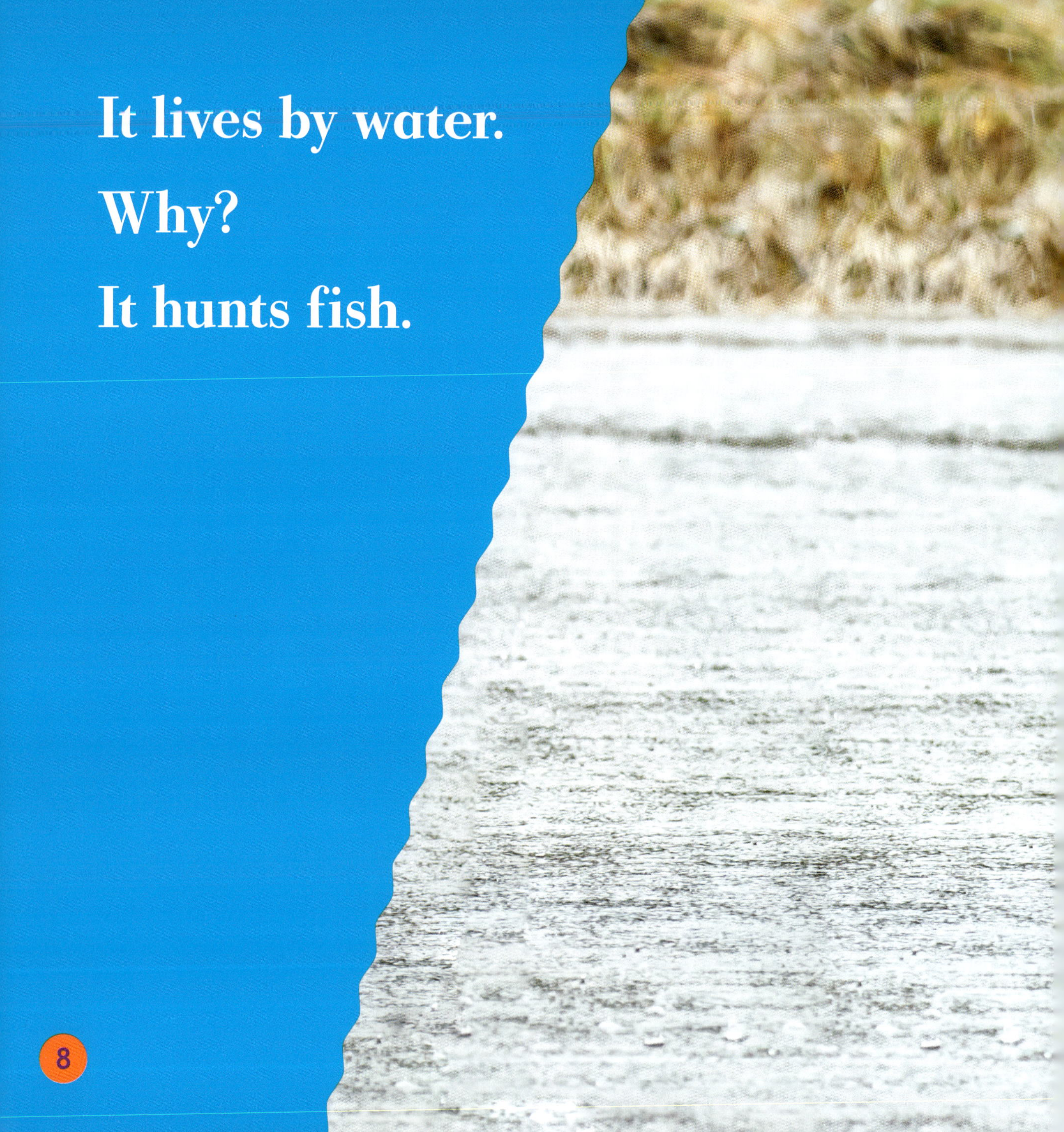

It lives by water.

Why?

It hunts fish.

It sees one.

It flies down.

Splash!

The eagle has sharp talons.
They help it catch food.

The eagle has
a sharp beak.

It tears food.

The eagle eats.

beak

Bald eagles make big nests.

A mom lays eggs.

Chicks hatch.

They are gray.

A chick grows up!

It turns brown.

Now it is an adult.
It has a white head!

Parts of a Bald Eagle

What are the parts of a bald eagle? Take a look!

Picture Glossary

chicks
Young birds.

hatch
To break out of an egg.

hunts
Chases and kills animals for food.

tears
Pulls apart.

Index

To Learn More

Finding more information is as easy as 1, 2, 3.

1. Go to www.factsurfer.com
2. Enter "baldeagles" into the search box.
3. Choose your book to see a list of websites.